The
MOON
ALMANAC

THE MOON ALMANAC

Copyright © Summersdale Publishers Ltd, 2021

Illustrations by Alisha Gronska

An Hachette UK Company
www.hachette.co.uk

Summersdale Publishers Ltd
Part of Octopus Publishing Group Limited
Carmelite House
50 Victoria Embankment
LONDON
EC4Y 0DZ
UK

www.summersdale.com

Printed and bound in China

ISBN: 978-1-78783-991-5

Substantial discounts on bulk quantities of Summersdale books are available to corporations, professional associations and other organizations. For details contact general enquiries: telephone: +44 (0) 1243 771107 or email: enquiries@summersdale.com.

The
MOON
ALMANAC

*A Month-by-Month Guide
to the Lunar Year*

JUDITH HURRELL

summersdale

CONTENTS

INTRODUCTION

What is an Almanac?

Almanacs are essentially expanded calendars containing notes about what happens at a given time of year – they have a history as old as astronomy. Ancient Egyptians recorded lucky and unlucky dates and predictions about the weather on papyrus calendars. In ancient Rome, *fasti* (chronological lists) were used to chart lawful business days. For the medieval laity, snippets of psalms alongside calendars of religious feasts and saints' days were recorded in elaborately illustrated volumes known as psalters that offered jumping-off points for contemplation.

With the advent of the printing press, the almanac evolved into a form of folk literature containing fascinating miscellanea, seasonal suggestions, traditional remedies, jokes, verse and fiction alongside timely observations on the climate, seasonal rhythms and astronomical phenomena. With something for everyone and every mood, modern almanacs still have a special place on the bedside table, fireside shelf or potting shed bench.

How to Use this Book

This lunar companion brings together an eclectic collection of lunar lore, wisdom and trivia, with perspectives on the moon from poets, writers and philosophers from all corners of the globe and history. There's a moon for every mood and month.

There's no expectation for the book to be read in one sitting or from cover-to-cover – though of course, you may enjoy doing so. Instead, it's a book to come back to little and often, when the pull of the moon takes you. Dip into its pages with the changing of the seasons. Read it by torchlight while camping under the stars, curled up in bed while glimpsing the moon through the curtains or in the garden while planning your veg patch. Satisfy your curiosity about our nearest natural satellite and discover how the moon has been celebrated and revered throughout history the world over, and continues to be an inspiration today. From predicting the weather and moon gardening to inspiring poetry and romance, following the moon's rhythms and changing face will bring a new perspective to your month, and carry you through the year with a deeper connection to the cosmos.

PHASES OF THE MOON

The moon circles the Earth, just as the Earth orbits the sun. This perpetual dance means the geometry of the moon keeps changing from the Earth's perspective.

Like all planets, the moon doesn't make light. As the moon orbits the Earth, it's lit by the sun and the glow we see coming from the moon is a reflection of this light. A small amount of the light also comes from distant stars and the reflection of light from the Earth (known as earthshine).

Half of the moon is always lit by the sun – except during a lunar eclipse – but we see different parts. These changing aspects are known as moon "phases". These patterns of light progress as follows:

- **New Moon** – The moon is between the Earth and the sun, so its far side is lit up, and the side facing the Earth is in darkness.

- **Waxing Crescent Moon** – The moon's illuminated hemisphere is still facing mostly away from Earth, so we see only a slender fraction.

- **First Quarter Moon** – The moon is one-quarter of the way around its orbit of Earth, so is showing us half of its lighted half.

- **Waxing Gibbous Moon** – A large and growing section of the moon's illuminated hemisphere faces our way.

- **Full Moon** – The sun and the moon are aligned on opposite sides of Earth, so its Earth-side is fully lit up.

- **Waning Gibbous Moon** – A large but shrinking section of the moon's illuminated hemisphere faces our way.

- **Third Quarter Moon** – The moon is three-quarters of the way around its orbit of the Earth, so is showing us half of its bright half. This half is the opposite of that seen in the first quarter.

- **Waning Crescent Moon** – The moon is moving between the Earth and the sun, so is showing us less and less of its lit side.

- **Dark Moon** – The moon is between the Earth and the sun, so its far side is lit up and the side facing the Earth is in darkness.

One full cycle takes approximately 29.5 days, before beginning again.

Chapter 1

January's Moon

Make a super start to the new year – January is the perfect time to spot a Crescent Moon in the early evening twilight.

WOLVES, QUIET NIGHTS AND HOLIDAYS

The Wolf Moon – so-called by Europeans, Wiccans and Native Americans – takes its name from the lupine howling that peaks during the mid-winter breeding season. It's a myth that wolves howl at the moon, but they are more likely to howl at twilight, pointing their snouts toward the sky as they do so.

— ☾ —

Traditional wisdom said wolves were howling in hunger. However, a study of wolves from two packs living at Austria's Wolf Science Center suggests wolves howl because they care – they are more likely to howl at a fellow wolf they have a bond with.

Native Americans had a healthy sense of respect – rather than fear – for wolves. As North America's dominant carnivore, wolves were revered for their hunting skills, bravery and pack loyalty – traits the tribes saw in themselves.

— ☾ —

January's moon was also known as Old Moon, which may derive from the phrase "Old Fellow" – once a common nickname for winter. Ancient Greeks and Old World Pagans often personified the seasons in their mythology, literature and popular culture.

— ☾ —

In China, January's moon is called the Holiday Moon – Chinese New Year often falls in January, although the date varies according to the Chinese lunar calendar. This high point in the year, also known as the Spring Festival or Lunar New Year, is the grandest festival in China. Festivities begin on the New Moon and continue for 15 days, culminating on the Full Moon with a dazzling lantern festival.

Celtic traditions refer to January's moon as the Quiet Moon, due to the hushed winter landscape that was often cloaked in snow.

— ☾ —

Pagan traditions named January's moon the Ice Moon due to weather conditions in the Northern hemisphere at this time of year.

— ☾ —

In New Guinea, they call January's moon the Rainbow Fish Moon – perhaps because this moon coincides with the colourful native fish's spawning season.

— ☾ —

In the Southern hemisphere, January's moon is called the Thunder Moon, the Rumble Moon or the Lightning Moon after the storms that are common at this time of year.

The whole moon and the entire sky are reflected in one dewdrop on the grass.

DŌGEN

THE CRESCENT MOON

January is an excellent time to spot a young Crescent Moon. In the first quarter or last quarter of the moon's cycle, only a slither of its surface is illuminated by the sun, creating a crescent or sickle shape.

— ☾ —

When the moon is waxing (during the first half of a lunar month, when the moon's visible section is getting bigger), its crescent tip always points away from sunset. Very young waxing Crescent Moons hover just above the western horizon at twilight.

— ☾ —

When the moon is waning (during the latter half of a lunar month, when the moon's visible section is getting smaller), at around 23 days into its cycle, it appears crescent-like again for five days. During this phase, the moon rises in the dawn twilight of the eastern sky with its tips pointing toward sunrise.

Crescent Moons always hang low in the sky and are confined to dawn or dusk; they're never visible in complete darkness.

The orientation of the crescent depends on the time, the season and the viewer's location. In the Northern hemisphere from January until March, the moon can appear as a benevolent smile during the evening twilight.

In January, the path of the moon tracks vertically upward from the sunset point. During the rest of the year, the Crescent Moon traces the horizon on a leftward slant, making it more challenging to spot due to hazy horizons. Crescent Moons can be almost impossible to see during autumn.

THE INVISIBLE MOON

When the sun and moon are aligned, with the sun and Earth on opposite sides of the moon, we call this a New Moon. Because the sunlit side of the moon is facing away from the Earth, brand-new moons are not usually visible from our terrestrial perspective. It's rare to see any sign of the moon in the 24 hours either side of a New Moon.

— ☽ —

It has long been a sport among amateur astronomers to spot the youngest moon possible. In 1916, two British housemaids claimed to have seen a New Moon at only 14 and three-quarter hours old. A more widely accepted record was achieved in 1990 by Stephen James O'Meara, a visual astronomer, whose observational prowess is world renowned: he spotted a young Crescent Moon with his naked eye at just 15 hours and 32 minutes old.

— ☽ —

The wire-slim crescent of a one-day-old January moon is slightly more visible. It will appear, illuminated by earthshine, for a brief interval after sunset. At two days old, the moon should become easier to spot, appearing higher on the horizon around 15 minutes after sunset.

January's Moon in Literature

The sunset embers smoulder low,
The Moon climbs o'er the hill,
The peaks have caught the alpenglow,
The robin's song is still.

JOHN L. STODDARD,
FROM "GRATITUDE"

I saw the moon
One windy night,
Flying so fast –
All silvery white –
Over the sky
Like a toy balloon
Loose from its string –
A runaway Moon.
The frosty stars
Went racing past,
Chasing her on
Ever so fast.
Then everyone said,
"It's the clouds that fly,
And the stars and the moon
Stand still in the sky."
But I don't mind –
I saw the Moon
Sailing away
Like a toy
Balloon.

J. M. WESTRUP,
"FLYING"

Slipping softly through the sky
Little horned, happy moon,
Can you hear me up so high?
Will you come down soon?

On my nursery window-sill
Will you stay your steady flight?
And then float away with me
Through the summer night?

Brushing over tops of trees,
Playing hide and seek with stars,
Peeping up through shiny clouds
At Jupiter or Mars.

I shall fill my lap with roses
Gathered in the milky way,
All to carry home to mother.
Oh! what will she say!

Little rocking, sailing moon,
Do you hear me shout – Ahoy!
Just a little nearer, moon,
To please a little boy.

AMY LOWELL,
"THE CRESCENT MOON"

HUSBANDS, BAD WEATHER AND SMILES

An old West Sussex superstition held that a New Moon was a good time for girls to visualize their future husband. Curious girls were advised to sit across a gate or stile and look at the first New Moon that rose after New Year's Day. They were to go alone and in secret, chanting:

All hail to thee, moon, all hail to thee
I pray thee, good moon, reveal to me
This night who my husband must be.

It was believed that the face of the girl's future husband would come to her in a dream that night.

According to German folklore, wood should not be chopped during the "evil crescent" (a waxing moon). Firewood felled during this moon phase would not stay alight long.

Scottish folklore suggests a halo around the moon means bad weather is coming: "If the moon shows like a silver shield, You need not be afraid to reap your field, But if she rises haloed round, Soon we'll tread on deluged ground."

— ☾ —

Another Scottish saying predicts: "clear moon, frost soon".

— ☾ —

Cornish wisdom states that "a fog and a small moon brings an easterly wind soon".

The day, water, sun, moon, night – I do not have to purchase these things with money.

PLAUTUS

THE SMILING MOON

Is the moon smiling at you? Next time you catch sight of a Crescent Moon at twilight in January, February or March, notice how it's tilted on its back, to resemble a smile. This moon is sometimes called a Cheshire Moon, after the smile of the Cheshire Cat in Lewis Carroll's *Alice in Wonderland*.

Hawaiian mythology refers to this moon as a Wet Moon. This isn't because of any actual water on the moon or any watery influence on Earth, rather it's because this moon resembles a bowl holding water. In Hawaiian Astrology, Kaelo the Water Bearer reigns from 20 January to 18 February. During that time, the Wet Moon becomes the Dripping Wet Moon – the bowl overflows with water causing summer rains.

The opposite applies on autumn evenings and spring mornings: the moon's crescent is upright, making it incapable of holding any water. This is a Dry Moon.

Other Hawaiian stories swap these definitions around – imagining the moon holding water back from Earth when it's on its back, and pouring water over us when it's upright.

A Wet and Dry Moon are both Crescent Moons, but they sit at different angles to the horizon. Because the Earth's tilt changes relative to the plane on which the moon orbits, the angle of the Crescent Moon also changes.

✦ *Did you know?* ✦

The moon doesn't make its own light – without the sun it would be a dull orb in the sky. The moonlight we see is a reflection of sunlight hitting the moon – the moon reflects between three and 12 per cent of the sunlight it receives.

✦ *Did you know?* ✦

Until the Apollo space program, scientists didn't know how the moon was formed. Some thought it was a wandering body that was captured by the Earth's gravity in passing. Others believed the moon was created at the same time as Earth; another theory proposed the moon was a spin-off fragment of Earth.

Astronauts from NASA's Apollo missions brought back over 2,000 samples of rock and soil from the moon. Study of this material continues to reveal information about the history of the moon, the Earth and the early solar system. Investigation suggests that the Earth and moon have a linked history and share chemical characteristics. This gave rise to a theory that the moon and Earth were born following a giant collision between an early proto-Earth and a Mars-sized planet called Theia. During this colossal crash – around four and a half billion years ago – most of Earth and Theia melted and mutated into Earth, with a small part spinning off to form the moon. This "giant-impact theory" is now the most accepted explanation of how the moon was created.

Chapter 2

February's Moon

Fall in love under February's
moon and perhaps celebrate the
beginning of a lunar New Year.

ICE, BONES AND BUDDING

In Celtic tradition, February's Full Moon is known as the Moon of Ice, in a nod to the weather, or the Rowan Moon – after the rowan tree, which was also associated with the Celtic goddess of Brigit, Brigid or Bríg. This fire goddess stood watch over mothers and families and kept hearth fires burning. She is still celebrated today, on the first of February, at the Imbolc festival, when people weave Brigit's crosses from rushes. Representations of the goddess are also found in straw or corn Bridey dolls that were crafted and placed next to the fireplace, to welcome light and fortune to the home.

The cold, snowy weather in North America earned February's Full Moon the name Snow Moon. In Native American Cherokee tradition, this moon is called the Bone Moon. It gets its name from the time of the year when animal bones were their only food source. This moon is also a time to commune with dead ancestors.

Empty bellies in other North American tribes meant this moon was called the Hunger Moon by the Kalapuya and the Little Famine Moon by the Choctaw.

— ☾ —

February's Full Moon often acts as the pinnacle of the Lunar New Year festivities in China, which begin on the previous New Moon – however, because the festival is determined by the lunar cycle, sometimes it falls in January. Its appearance will be celebrated with lantern parades, dragon dances, fireworks and festival food including *yuan xiao*, which translates as "first evening". These glutinous rice balls stuffed with a sweet paste are shaped like the Full Moon.

— ☾ —

In Korea, the fifteenth day after the Lunar New Year triggers the Daeboreum festival. The moon's beams are believed to banish darkness, disease and misfortune. It's a Korean tradition to brave freezing temperatures and climb mountains to view this moon. The first person to see it is thought to enjoy good luck all year.

Those are the same stars,
and that is the same moon,
that look down upon your
brothers and sisters, and
which they see as they
look up to them, though
they are ever so far away
from us, and each other.

SOJOURNER TRUTH

FALL IN LOVE UNDER THE MOON

One Chinese legend speaks of a man in the moon who unites lovers with an invisible silk ribbon. When the time is right for them to fall in love, he draws the ribbons together. Astrologers still look at moon signs to determine the compatibility of star signs.

— ☾ —

Translated as "The moon is beautiful, is it not?" the phrase *Tsuki ga kirei, desu ne?* is code for "I love you" in Japan. Legend has it the expression dates back to the Meiji era. Novelist and teacher, Natsume Soseki – a product of the reserved, inhibited culture of the time – suggested two people in love didn't need words to make their feelings understood. At a time when lovers couldn't even hold hands in public, the phrase took on a more subtle, nuanced meaning, which is still used in Japanese manga comics today.

February's Moon in Literature

Thick draws the dark,
And spark by spark,
The frost-fires kindle, and soon
Over that sea of frozen foam
Floats the white moon.

WALTER DE LA MARE,
FROM "WINTER"

The Moon's a snowball. See the drifts
Of white that cross the sphere.
The Moon's a snowball, melted down
A dozen times a year.

Yet rolled again in hot July
When all my days are done
And cool to greet the weary eye
After the scorching sun.

The moon's a piece of winter fair
Renewed the year around,
Behold it, deathless and unstained,
Above the grimy ground!

It rolls on high so brave and white
Where the clear air-rivers flow,
Proclaiming Christmas all the time
And the glory of the snow!

VACHEL LINDSAY,
"WHAT THE SNOW MAN SAID"

White in the moon the long road lies,
The moon stands blank above;
White in the moon the long road lies
That leads me from my love.

Still hangs the hedge without a gust,
Still, still the shadows stay:
My feet upon the moonlit dust
Pursue the ceaseless way.

The world is round, so travellers tell,
And straight though reach the track,
Trudge on, trudge on, 'twill all be well,
The way will guide one back.

But ere the circle homeward hies
Far, far must it remove:
White in the moon the long road lies
That leads me from my love.

A. E. HOUSMAN,
"XXXVI"

RELIGION AND MYTHOLOGY

The American tradition of Groundhog Day grew from a Roman custom carried out under a clear February Moon. The ancient Romans watched hedgehogs emerging from their burrows during this month. If they cast a shadow under a clear moon, this was believed to signal six more weeks of winter.

— ☾ —

For Inuit people, Alignak is the god of the moon and weather, presiding over the tides, earthquakes and eclipses. He dwells in harbours, protecting fishermen from the wrath of the sea goddess.

— ☾ —

For the ancient Greeks, Artemis was the goddess of the moon and hunting, and was often depicted beside a Crescent Moon. Her Roman counterpart was Diana. Like Artemis, the goddess Diana was a hunter whose light-bearing power was associated with the moon. Riding a silver chariot and armed with silver arrows in a silver bow, she protects labouring women, children and wild animals.

— ☾ —

Selene – whose Roman equivalent is Luna – is the only Greek goddess to be portrayed as the moon incarnate by early classical poets. When her lover, Endymion, was cursed with eternal sleep, Selene descended from the sky every night to sleep beside him. She was celebrated during the Full Moon. The word "selenophile", meaning "moon lover", is derived from the goddess's name.

— ☾ —

In Celtic mythology, Cerridwen was the keeper of the cauldron of knowledge – a font of wisdom and inspiration. She's often associated with the moon due to her powers of intuition. As the ruler of the dark and hidden realm, the moon has long been linked to the subconscious and intuition.

— ☾ —

In Chinese folklore, the moon is the embodiment of Chang'e, the wife of the tyrannical king, Hou Yi, who sacrificed herself for the sake of her people and flew to the moon. Her story is still told to this day, as an example of self-sacrifice for the benefit of others.

— ☾ —

In Aztec mythology, the moon is the head of Coyolxauhqui, a beautiful young woman who was beheaded by her brother Huitzilopochtli.

Legend has it that an ancient Egyptian god of the moon, Khonsu, gambled with the moon's light in a game against Thoth, god of wisdom, writing, magic, medicine and the moon. Thoth won enough moonlight to add five days to the month. These five days were added to the end of the year, bringing the Egyptian calendar of 360 days in line with the solar year of 365 days. The name Khonsu means "traveller" and may be related to the passage of the moon across the sky.

— ☾ —

In one Hawaiian folktale, a beautiful cloth-maker, Hina, fashioned soft cloth from the bark of the banyan tree. Tired of working long hours with no help from her husband and sons, she left Earth via a rainbow to the sun. But the sun was too hot, so she hitched a ride on a rainbow to the moon, where she made her home. The Hawaiian name for the moon, *mahina*, is derived from her name.

— ☾ —

The Hindu god, Soma, was thought to embody the moon. He was also the keeper of an elixir of mortality. When the moon waned, the gods were blamed for drinking the potion. In the Hindu calendar, *Ēkādaśī*, or *Ēkādaśi*, is the eleventh day after a New Moon and the eleventh day after a Full Moon. These days are thought to be ideal for cleansing and fasting to rejuvenate the body. According to Hindu scriptures, the mind is swayed by the moon. The bearing of the moon during *Ēkādaśī* is said to boost concentration for worship and meditation.

✦ *Did you know?* ✦

It would take around 17 days of continuous flight to get to the moon on a commercial plane. The moon is orbiting Earth at an average distance of 238,855 miles (384,400 kilometres) – this is the distance of about 30 Earths.

Because the moon's orbit is elliptical, this distance varies. When the moon is at its farthest point from Earth, it's approximately 252,088 miles (405,696 kilometres) away – or the distance of about 32 Earths. When it's at its closest point to Earth, the moon is about 225,623 (363,105 kilometres) miles away – the distance of between 28 and 29 Earths.

If the Sun & Moon

should Doubt,

They'd immediately

Go out.

WILLIAM BLAKE

Chapter 3

March's Moon

This month, mark the Spring Equinox
(20 March): a harbinger of spring
in the Northern hemisphere.

WORMS, CROWS AND RISING SAP

In Old England, March's moon was called the Lenten Moon, after Lent. In astronomical terms, it's the last Full Moon of winter in a tropical year – the time it takes for the sun to make one complete cycle of the seasons and return to the same position.

— ☾ —

Native South Americans called this moon the Worm Moon, after earthworms that would emerge at this time of year, leaving lacy trails on the newly thawed ground.

— ☾ —

On the other hand, some North American tribes gave this moon the moniker Crow Moon, after the cawing of crows that signalled the coming of spring.

Other tribes called this moon the Crust Moon after the layer of crunchy snow that formed as it thawed during the day and refroze overnight.

March was also a time for the Shawnee tribe to tap maple trees for sap, giving this moon the name Sap Moon. The Tewa Pueblo tribe named it the Moon When the Leaves Break Forth.

— ☾ —

Other names include Chaste Moon, symbolizing the purity of early spring.

— ☾ —

Indian Spring

In India, the Full Moon in March usually coincides with the festival of Holi, celebrated on the last Full Moon during the lunar month of Phalgun. In this riotous event, revellers throw brightly coloured powders over each other to celebrate the beginning of spring and honour the triumph of good over evil.

March's Moon in Literature

In the black furrow of a field
I saw an old witch-hare this night;
And she cocked her lissome ear,
And she eyed the moon so bright,
And she nibbled o' the green;
And I whispered "Whsst! witch-hare,"
Away like a ghostie o'er the field
She fled, and left the moonlight there.

WALTER DE LA MARE,
"THE HARE"

The Moon is distant from the Sea –
And yet, with Amber Hands –
She leads Him – docile as a Boy –
Along appointed Sands –

He never misses a Degree –
Obedient to Her eye –
He comes just so far – toward the Town –
Just so far – goes away –

Oh, Signor, Thine, the Amber Hand –
And mine – the distant Sea –
Obedient to the least command
Thine eye impose on me –

EMILY DICKINSON,
"THE MOON IS DISTANT
FROM THE SEA"

Owl of the hollow tree,
Speaking mysteriously,
When the moon's phantom light
Makes my dim chamber bright.

DOROTHEA MARIA OGILVY,
FROM "THE OWL"

— ☾ —

The evening river is level and motionless—
The spring colours just open to their full.
Suddenly a wave carries the moon away
And the tidal water comes with its
    freight of stars.

YANG-TI,
"FLOWERS AND MOONLIGHT
ON THE SPRING RIVER"

MOON-GAZING
HARES AND RABBITS

Cultures all over the world have linked the moon to the hare.

— ☾ —

The universal symbol of the moon-gazing hare has ancient origins. As a symbol of fertility, Pagans believed moon-gazing hares brought growth, rebirth, abundance and new beginnings. Some even thought they had divination powers. In 60 CE, before leading her army into battle with the Romans, the Iceni rebel queen, Boudica, released a hare from the folds of her dress, believing it foretold victory.

— ☾ —

While Western cultures see a man in the moon, many others see a hare or rabbit. In China, the Moon's Hare – a protector of wild animals – is thought to be mixing an elixir of immortality with a mortar and pestle. In Chinese folklore, the touch of moonlight is believed to cause a female hare – or jill – to fall pregnant. The jill could also become pregnant by crossing a river by moonlight or licking moonlight from a male hare's fur.

For the Aztecs, the rabbit or hare in the moon offered himself up as food for the hungry god, Quetzalcoatl. The moon was so grateful it painted a tribute to the animal on its surface.

— ☽ —

In Egyptian mythology the waning moon was seen as masculine, and the waxing moon was seen as feminine. Hares were also believed to shift genders according to this cycle.

— ☽ —

For the Ugric people of Western Siberia, Kaltes was a shape-shifting moon goddess who took the form of a hare when roaming the hills. In human form, she was depicted wearing a headdress with hare's ears.

— ☽ —

In Britain, the ancient tradition of the Easter Bunny dates back to Anglo-Saxon times. Legend has it that the Easter Bunny decorates and hides chocolate eggs for children to find in an Easter egg hunt.

Ēostre, the pagan goddess of the moon, fertility and spring, was often depicted with a hare's head and ears. Her magical companion, a white hare, gave out coloured eggs to children during spring fertility festivals.

March is an ideal time to spot March hares "boxing" on their hind legs, as part of their mating dance. A rare sighting under the equinox moonlight is said to be lucky.

Where, indeed, does the moon not look well? What is the scene, confined or expansive, which her orb does not hallow?

CHARLOTTE BRONTË

THE MOON AND NATURE

The moon plays conductor for many rhythms in nature. Plants and animals take cues from the push and pull of the tides, the shifts in light and the moon's arc across the horizon.

— ☾ —

Barau's petrel, an endangered seabird that breeds on the island of Réunion in the Indian Ocean, synchronizes its migration with the Full Moon. Masses of these birds arrive at their breeding ground on the night of the Full Moon every year.

— ☾ —

The flowerless Ephedra plant has adapted to use moonbeams to lure pollinators. Its cones produce sticky droplets that sparkle under the Full Moon's polarized light, attracting beetles and other nocturnal insects.

— ☾ —

Polarized light also helps African dung beetles to navigate in a straight line. When Swedish scientists studied dung beetles under non-polarized, artificial laboratory lights, the disorientated beetles walked in circles.

The mass spawning of corals on the Great Barrier Reef is also triggered by the moon. The corals contain photosensitive molecules that respond to moonlight. The sight of billions of coral polyps drifting to the water's surface like an upside-down snow globe is so dramatic that it can even be seen from space.

— ☾ —

As keen orienteers, sandhoppers use the moon to avoid being washed out to sea or stranded on the beach, where they might dry up. They rely on a "moon compass" in their antennae and a "sun compass" in their brain to commute between the sand and the water, foraging at night during low tide.

— ☾ —

Male sand fiddler crabs benefit from a more powerful snapping claw during a Full and New Moon; vital for attracting females and battling with rivals. Scientists believe their mighty snap could be motivated by the abundance of females searching for a mate during these moon phases. Female crabs time the delivery of their babies according to the most powerful tidal flux. When the moon is full or new, the resulting tides are more likely to sweep the larvae to safety.

Adult prairie rattlesnakes keep a low profile on moonlit nights, perhaps to avoid hunting predators but also due to the activity patterns of their nocturnal rodent prey. Brown tree snakes only slide down from their tree canopies on New Moon nights for similar reasons.

— ☾ —

The ovaries of sea urchins swell during a Full Moon thanks to a cycle of growth and development that corresponds with the moon throughout the breeding season. Some scientists believe that sticking to strict reproductive rhythms maximizes the chances of fertilization and prevents cross-species reproduction.

— ☾ —

Most bats keep their heads down during bright moonlit nights, staying tucked up in their roosts. Common vampire bats are most active during New Moon nights and darker periods. Their activity is influenced by the risks posed by predators, or the availability of their prey.

Moonstruck owl monkeys and red-fronted lemurs often pull all-nighters on Full Moon nights – except on cloudy nights or during eclipses, when they sleep in. Research suggests they favour moonlit nights because they find them easier to forage for food.

— ☾ —

For a few nights during summer, the British lapwing – usually a daylight hunter – shakes up its bedtime routine. During Full Moon nights in summer, it roosts by day and feeds by night. Some studies suggest that lapwings are opportunists who take advantage of an abundance of prey during these nights. Others suggest the lapwings change their behaviour due to roosting conditions: lapwings roost on dry ground, in the open, where they're vulnerable to attacks from owls and foxes. On brightly lit nights in summer it may be safer for them to roost during the day.

— ☾ —

British night-migrating skylarks wait for a waxing Gibbous Moon to illuminate the sky for almost a week, as they fly to Southern Europe and North Africa each winter. The moon illuminates the horizon best during this phase, helping the birds take navigational clues from the landscape.

Doodlebugs – the larvae of antlions – catch their prey by digging and crouching in funnel-shaped holes in their sandy landscapes. Research shows they dig deeper and broader traps during Full Moons. Scientists assumed doodlebugs were trying to take advantage of the increase in prey activity during full moon nights. However a discovery that this habit persists even in the complete darkness of a laboratory suggests the lunar cycle could also play a role.

Brightly moonlit nights can mean less prey for night-time hunting lions. This means lions are at their hungriest following a Full Moon. In rural Africa there is a spike in lion attacks on humans during this time: in the nights following a Full Moon, the moon doesn't appear in the sky until well after dark. During these long dark evenings humans are still active. Hungry lions are more likely to prey on humans to catch up on missed meals.

Did you know that scorpions glow in the dark? Because armour, pinchers and poisonous stingers aren't freaky enough, right? Scientists are undecided about why the arachnids are equipped with a protein that reacts with the UV rays of moonlight. Still, they have noticed that scorpions are busiest during the New Moon and take cover on Full Moon nights – perhaps due to their fluorescence.

— ☾ —

Female terrestrial crabs, living high in the mountains above the Ogamo River in Japan, only make the journey to the sea to release their eggs during a spring tide's New or Full Moon.

— ☾ —

For the Euroasian badger, the New Moon means romance: matings are highest during these long dark nights.

— ☾ —

Hamsters get sporty on Full Moon nights. A four-year study found that hamsters spun their wheels more during and just after a Full Moon.

There is a moon inside

every human being. Learn

to be companions with it.

RUMI

Tree stem diameters fluctuate with the tide, suggesting that the moon influences the flow of water between different parts of trees.

Lunar Retreat

The moon is steadily moving further away from Earth. Astronauts from the Apollo missions and two Soviet Union remote-controlled rovers left mirrors on the surface of the moon, which allow astronomers on Earth to bounce laser beams off the moon and calculate the distance between the two bodies.

— ☾ —

The retreat of the moon away from our planet is mainly down to the Earth's tides. The moon maintains its orbit thanks to a gravitational force exerted by our planet. However, the moon also has a gravitational force on Earth, pulling the water in our oceans toward it in a tidal bulge. Because the Earth spins faster than the moon orbits around it, the bulge sits slightly ahead of the moon. This boosts the moon's orbit, pushing it higher.

A similar phenomenon can be felt on a children's roundabout: the faster the roundabout spins the stronger the feeling of being swung outward.

The same process is also causing Earth's rotation to slow and the length of day to increase. As the Earth rotates beneath the tidal bulges, it attempts to drag the bulges along with it. A large amount of friction is produced, which slows down the Earth's spin.

— ☾ —

Scientists have discovered the moon is migrating at around 3.78 cm (1.49 inches) a year – roughly the speed at which our fingernails grow. They refer to this as "lunar retreat" and believe, at the time of its formation, the moon was only around 14,000 miles (22,530 kilometres) away, compared with the 238,855 miles (384,399 kilometres) between the Earth and the moon today.

— ☾ —

While this speed of migration doesn't seem much, over a long period it could make our planet slow down, influencing life on Earth. The world could become unstable, which would magnify the seasons. Certain parts of the world could experience extreme temperature swings with freezing Arctic temperatures in winter followed by blazing hot temperatures in summer. But we don't need to lose any sleep yet; this would take billions of years, and may never happen at all.

Chapter 4

April's Moon

April is a great time to channel the fertility of the season and sow a moon garden. Worried about April showers? Discover why it's best to take cover if you spot a moon halo...

NEW SHOOTS AND EGGS

The Celts called April's Full Moon the Growing Moon, the Budding Moon, the New Shoots Moon or the Seed Moon, while the Anglo Saxons named it the Egg Moon; all reflections of the season.

— ☾ —

The widespread pink wild ground phlox flowers that bloomed in Northern Native American lands during April inspired the name, Pink Moon.

— ☾ —

A night-time navigator

The dark can be disorientating, but on a clear night, with the moon high, help is at hand. Next time you're lost in the dark, try extending a line from the horns of a Crescent Moon to the horizon. In northern latitudes, this will point roughly south.

Watching the Full Moon rise or set can also help you find your whereabouts. A Full Moon is directly opposite the sun and moves in the opposite direction. So, in the Northern hemisphere it comes up in the southeast in midsummer and northwest in midwinter. At midnight it will be close to due south. In the Southern hemisphere, although the Full Moon still rises in an easterly direction and sets in a westerly direction, it arcs across the northern sky, crossing due north at midnight.

April's Moon in Literature

Oh, well the world is dreaming
Under the April moon,
Her soul in love with beauty,
Her senses all a-swoon!

Pure hangs the silver crescent
Above the twilight wood,
And pure the silver music
Wakes from the marshy flood.

O Earth, with all thy transport,
How comes it life should seem
A shadow in the moonlight,
A murmur in a dream?

BLISS CARMAN,
"UNDER THE APRIL MOON"

As the stars draw back their shining faces
when they surround the fair moon in her
silver fullness.

SAPPHO,
FROM "AWED BY HER SPLENDOUR"

— ☾ —

I see the moon, the moon sees me,
God bless the moon and God bless me:
There's grace in the cottage and grace
  in the hall;
And the grace of God is over us all.

OLD IRISH FOLK SONG

Did you see the rainy moon
Up above the roofs last night?
It was like a primrose flower
When the mist is blowing white,

When a film of gossamer
Flutters from the evening tree,
And the primroses are pale
And the dusk has come to be.

I should like to go with you
Past the primrose-haunted mist
To that hill among the clouds
Where we trembled, where we kissed.

GRACE HAZARD CONKLING,
"THE RAINY MOON"

The child's wonder
At the old moon
Comes back nightly.
She points her finger
To the far silent yellow thing
Shining through the branches
Filtering on the leaves a golden sand,
Crying with her little tongue,
   "See the moon!"
And in her bed fading to sleep
With babblings of the moon on her
   little mouth.

CARL SANDBURG,
"CHILD MOON"

RAIN, SOWING SEEDS AND
TENDING A MOON GARDEN

The moon and the weather
May change together;
But change of the moon
Does not change the weather;
If we'd no moon at all,
And that may seem strange,
We still should have weather
That's subject to change.

ENGLISH PROVERB

Can the moon hold off the rain? Folklore passed on by sailors has long suggested that the Full Moon "eats clouds". An old shepherd's proverb also states "The circle of the moon never filled a pond", meaning it doesn't often rain during a Full Moon. Science has recently confirmed that when the Full Moon rises, it creates a bulge in the Earth's atmosphere, meaning higher pressure and a rise in temperatures. This in turn makes rain less likely.

Other cultures link the appearance of the moon to rain. Zulu wisdom holds that "If the Moon's face is red, of water she speaks." In 1670, John Claridge published *The Shepherd of Banbury's Rules to Judge of the Changes of the Weather*, which states: "Sudden rains never last long; but when the air grows thick by degrees, and the sun, moon, and stars shine dimmer and dimmer, then it is likely to rain six hours usually."

— ☾ —

Meanwhile, John Clarke's book of English and Latin proverbs, published in 1639, states:

Pale Moon doth rain,
Red Moon doth blow.
White Moon doth neither
rain nor snow.

But do these proverbs hold any truth? Researchers at Washington University in the US have made the link between rain and the moon official. According to their study, the moon's gravitational pull not only influences the water in our seas, but also has an effect on the water in the clouds. This "atmospheric tide" causes the Earth's atmosphere to bulge toward the moon. The resulting air pressure causes the air to heat up. Because warm air can hold more water vapour than cooler air, the air beneath the moon is more likely to hang onto water that may otherwise have fallen as rain. So the amount of rainfall we get here on Earth is very slightly influenced by the moon.

— ☾ —

An adage from North America: "halo around the moon, rain soon" also bears true: the halo is caused by moisture in the atmosphere.

— ☾ —

Gardeners, be guided by the moon. In 1903 the United States Weather Bureau published this poem in a bulletin on *Weather Folk-Lore and Local Weather Signs*:

Plant your beans when the moon is light,
You will find that this is right;
Plant potatoes when the moon is dark,
And to this line you'll always hark;
But if you vary from this rule,
You will find you are a fool;
Follow this rule to the end.
And you'll have lots of dough to spend.

The age-old practise of sowing, tending and harvesting in tune with the moon dates back to the birth of agriculture. Back in the first century, the Roman naturalist, Pliny the Elder, noted that the moon "replenishes the Earth; when she approaches it, she fills all bodies, while, when she recedes, she empties them."

— ☾ —

Various moon-based gardening systems exist: the most popular is based on the moon's phases and the changing moonlight. Plant growth is linked to the increasing and decreasing light of the waxing and waning moon. So planting crops during the waxing phase and harvesting crops or cutting timber during the waning phase produces the best results. Refinements specify the ideal day to plant or harvest individual plants.

Other systems are based on the gravitational pull of the moon. These speculate that the moon affects the moisture in the earth, much like it affects the tides. The Full and New Moon act like magnets, pulling water to the surface of the soil, encouraging germination and growth.

— ☾ —

The most complicated system takes account of both the gravitational pull of the moon, its changing light and the position of the stars, dividing plants into zodiac signs.

— ☾ —

John Harris has been gardening according to the moon throughout his 30-year stint as head gardener at Tresillian House, near Newquay in Cornwall, UK. He follows the moon phases – planting root vegetables when the moisture is rising at the Full and New Moon. During the first quarter, John sows plants that crop above ground: corn, flowers and legumes. When the water table is at its lowest, during the last quarter of the moon cycle, he concentrates on digging, manuring, taking cuttings and pruning hedges.

"The moon's gravitational pull is felt by the land, the sea and the atmosphere and all the plants and the creatures that live therein. It is felt by the earth's water table, which lies beneath the land. This rises as the moon's pull increases and falls as the moon's pull decreases. The gardener who knows this and when during the 29-day cycle to work with these extremes will have a far greater knowledge of working in harmony with nature.

Have you ever bought supermarket fruit, only to be disappointed that it tastes like cardboard? I'd say this is at least partly down to a poorly-timed harvest. I was taught this early on during an eight-year apprenticeship with the head gardener at a lost estate in Newquay. Later, at Chelsea Flower Show, I got talking to a descendent of a Sioux Indian who was also a firm believer that following the cycles of the moon results in a better crop. Ancient wisdom from Native American, Incan,

Maori, Greek and Roman growers tells us they all cultivated in harmony with the moon cycle. Sowing at the optimum time, knowing what the plants need at each point in the moon's cycle and timing the harvest: these are the core principles around which I work. It's worth taking a step back occasionally and learning from what you see – in the garden and in life. Moon gardening encourages this, not to mention, yielding a better crop."

Planning some gardening this month? Why not plant some beetroot or carrot seeds around the New Moon? Nasturtiums and snapdragons will benefit from being planted during the first quarter.

With freedom, books,

flowers, and the moon,

who could not be happy?

OSCAR WILDE

Chapter 5

May's Moon

May 2022 brings a total lunar eclipse.
A spring eclipse is sometimes dubbed
a Total Blood Flower Moon eclipse,
due to its timing and reddish colour.

MILK AND FLOWERS

Old English cultures called May's Full Moon the Milk Moon, since farmers' cows would be suckling calves at this time and needed extra nourishment. On the first day of May, following the Beltane festival, they were moved to rich summer pastures.

— ☾ —

Moonrise on May Day eve was significant because it heralded the beginning of the Beltane festival for Anglo-Saxons and Celts. They celebrated the fertility of the land, the return of the light and the height of spring.

— ☾ —

Many cultures – such as the Native American Algonquin tribes – called May's Full Moon the Flower Moon, thanks to the abundance of flowers at this time of year.

— ☾ —

For some Celtic tribes, May's Full Moon was called the Hare Moon. To explore the ancient links between the moon and the hare, see chapter four on April's Moon.

WHAT IS A LUNAR ECLIPSE?

The moon's illumination comes from the reflected light of the sun. When the moon moves into the Earth's shadow – which only happens during a Full Moon, around three times a year – the sun's light is blocked, and a lunar eclipse occurs. There are three types of lunar eclipse: a partial eclipse, a penumbral eclipse and a total eclipse – with the latter being the most dramatic.

Partial Lunar Eclipse

When part of the moon travels through the Earth's umbra – the most defined part of the Earth's shadow – it appears to "take a bite" out of the moon. The dark bite grows and then shrinks as the moon moves. Some lunar eclipses are only ever partial, because the Earth and moon aren't perfectly aligned. Total lunar eclipses go through a partial phase either side of totality.

Penumbral Lunar Eclipse

When the lighter edge of the Earth's shadow – its penumbra – comes between the sun and the moon, the moon is subtly obscured. This type of eclipse is easily missed.

Total Lunar Eclipse

In this dramatic event, all three celestial bodies align in the sky to form a perfectly straight line. This means the moon is obscured by the darkest part of the Earth's umbra. While it won't disappear completely thanks to some scattered sunlight from the Earth's atmosphere, it will be cast into eerie darkness.

An Impossible Eclipse

This extremely rare cosmic wonder happens when the rising sun can be seen at the same time as a totally eclipsed moon. This is technically impossible according to celestial geometry, because the sun, moon and Earth are at 180 degrees during a total lunar eclipse. However, atmospheric refraction sometimes plays tricks. When the sun's light rays bend, they project an image of the rising sun on the eastern horizon ahead of its arrival. Likewise, they leave an impression of the setting moon in the western sky after it has set. This rare optical illusion is dubbed a "selenelin" or horizontal eclipse.

Why Does the Moon Appear Pink in a Lunar Eclipse?

When the Earth hovers between the sun and moon, it blocks the sun's light. The light that peeks around the edge of the Earth is refracted by its atmosphere. Because blue light bends and scatters more than red light, more red light reaches the moon, casting a pinkish glow. This is why a total lunar eclipse is often called a Blood Moon.

May's Moon in Literature

The spring is fresh and fearless
And every leaf is new,
The world is brimmed with moonlight,
The lilac brimmed with dew.

Here in the moving shadows
I catch my breath and sing –
My heart is fresh and fearless
And over-brimmed with spring.

SARA TEASDALE,
"MAY NIGHT"

The young May moon is beaming, love.
The glowworm's lamp is gleaming, love.
How sweet to rove
Through Morna's grove,
When the drowsy world is dreaming, love!
Then awake!—the heavens look bright,
   my dear.
'Tis never too late for delight, my dear.
And the best of all ways
To lengthen our days
Is to steal a few hours from the night,
   my dear.

THOMAS MOORE,
FROM "THE YOUNG MAY MOON"

There stood a Poplar, tall and straight;
The fair, round Moon, uprisen late,
Made the long shadow on the grass
A ghostly bridge 'twixt heaven and me.
But May, with slumbrous nights, must pass;
And blustering winds will strip the tree.
And I've no magic to express
The moment of that loveliness;
So from these words you'll never guess
The stars and lilies I could see.

SIEGFRIED SASSOON,
"A POPLAR AND THE MOON"

A black cat among roses,
Phlox, lilac-misted under a first-quarter moon,
The sweet smells of heliotrope and night-
    scented stock.
The garden is very still,
It is dazed with moonlight
Contented with perfume,
Dreaming the opium dreams of its
    folded poppies.

AMY LOWELL,
FROM "THE GARDEN BY MOONLIGHT"

BAD LUCK, POISON
AND KING SWAPS

Some Buddhists believe that the effects of good or bad deeds are magnified under a lunar eclipse – so behave!

— ☾ —

For the Batammaliba people of Togo and Benin, the eclipse is an ideal time to settle feuds. Traditional folk tales blame the eclipse on a quarrel between the sun and moon. It's up to the people on Earth to set a good example, and make peace.

— ☾ —

Christianity links lunar eclipses with the wrath of God, due to an eclipse reference during the crucifixion in the Bible. It is notable that Easter always falls on the first Sunday after the first Full Moon of spring, ensuring Easter can never coincide with an eclipse.

— ☾ —

Hindu superstition states that any food prepared during an eclipse will be poisonous, so it's bad luck to cook, eat or drink at this time.

The ancient Greeks feared an eclipse was an attack on their king. On the dreaded day, they would swap the real king for a stand-in. It was a short reign for the dummy: they would be executed once the moon returned to wholeness.

LUNAR LIES

Christopher Columbus used a lunar eclipse to manipulate the indigenous Arawak people when his crew were shipwrecked on Jamaica in 1503. Columbus and his stranded men needed food and shelter from the natives to survive. Despite a warm welcome, after six months, local generosity was waning.

When Columbus consulted his almanac, he noticed an eclipse was forecast for 29 February 1504, and decided to use it to his advantage. He warned the island's Chieftain that God would provide a clear sign that he was angry with the Arawak people for denying the sailors help. When the sky turned red, and the moon disappeared soon after, terror broke out among the islanders. Columbus held them to ransom, saying God would only forgive them if they kept the sailors fed. The Arawak people relented, and the sailors ate well until the next Spanish ship arrived.

Tell me what you feel in your room when the full moon is shining in upon you, and your lamp is dying out, and I will tell you how old you are, and I shall know if you are happy.

HENRI FRÉDÉRIC AMIEL

MOON DUST

Moon dust may sound magical, but it's dangerous stuff: the sharp fragments cut like glass. During Apollo missions, the dust ate through astronauts' moon boots, damaged their spacesuits and destroyed the seals on boxes used to bring samples back to Earth.

The moon is formed primarily of silicon dioxide: a product of billions of years of meteorite impacts on the moon's surface.

Astronaut Harrison (Jack) Schmitt accidentally inhaled lunar dust on the Apollo 17 mission. He said it smelled like gunpowder and it gave him "lunar hay fever". No one knows the actual effect of lunar dust on humans, but studies have revealed it causes cell death and DNA damage. Unfortunately for lunar explorers, avoiding moon dust is near impossible – the electrically-charged particles cling to everything they touch.

Chapter 6

June's Moon

Celebrate the shortest night and longest day of the year on the Summer Solstice (20 or 21 June in the UK). In Europe, due to discrepancies between the Julian calendar, the tropical year and the Gregorian calendar, Midsummer's Day is celebrated on 24 June.

STRAWBERRIES AND ROSES

Celts called June's Full Moon the Mead Moon, after the honey wine (or mead) that they brewed for wedding ceremonies at this time of year. Mead was believed to have aphrodisiac qualities, and they sometimes flavoured the drink with fruits, spices, grains or hops. The tradition of newlyweds drinking the honeyed wine after their nuptials gave rise to the term "honeymoon", which we still use today.

— ☾ —

The Algonquin tribes of eastern North America dubbed June's Full Moon the Strawberry Moon, after the wild strawberries that ripened during this month. Other tribes called this month's Full Moon the Buck Moon, in a nod to the male white-tailed deer who were often sprouting antlers at this time.

— ☾ —

Some Europeans called June's moon the Rose Moon, perhaps due to its rosy glow. Because this Full Moon takes a low arc through the sky, the earth's atmosphere often gives it a pinkish hue – much like during sunrise or sunset.

Roses have thorns,
and silver
fountains mud;
Clouds and eclipses
stain both
moon and sun,
And loathsome canker
lies in sweetest bud.

WILLIAM SHAKESPEARE

June's Moon in Literature

It is the hour when from the boughs
The nightingale's high note is heard;
It is the hour – when lover's vows
Seem sweet in every whisper'd word;
And gentle winds and waters near,
Make music to the lonely ear.
Each flower the dews have lightly wet,
And in the sky the stars are met,
And on the wave is deeper blue,
And on the leaf a browner hue,
And in the Heaven that clear obscure
So softly dark, and darkly pure,
That follows the decline of day
As twilight melts beneath the moon away.

LORD BYRON,
"IT IS THE HOUR"

She watched the moon, whose radiance stained with primrose the purple of the surrounding sky. In England the moon had seemed dead and alien; here she was caught in the shawl of night together with earth and all the other stars.

E. M. FORSTER,
FROM *A PASSAGE TO INDIA*

— ☾ —

I carry
The sun
In a golden cup.
The Moon
In a silver bag.

W. B. YEATS,
FROM "THOSE DANCING
DAYS ARE GONE"

Strange fits of passion have I known:
And I will dare to tell,
But in the lover's ear alone,
What once to me befell.

When she I loved look'd every day
Fresh as a rose in June,
I to her cottage bent my way,
Beneath an evening moon.

WILLIAM WORDSWORTH,
FROM "LUCY"

The Moon was but a Chin of Gold
A Night or two ago –
And now she turns Her perfect Face
Upon the World below –

Her Forehead is of Amplest Blonde –
Her Cheek – a Beryl hewn –
Her Eye unto the Summer Dew
The likest I have known –

Her Lips of Amber never part –
But what must be the smile
Upon Her Friend she could confer
Were such Her Silver Will –

EMILY DICKINSON,
FROM "THE MOON WAS
BUT A CHIN OF GOLD"

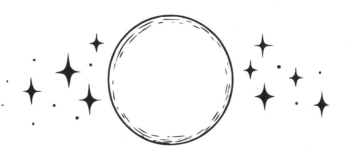

SUPER MOON

June's Full Moon in 2022 is dubbed a Super Moon, because from Earth it will appear bigger and brighter than at other times of year. The moon orbits Earth on an elliptical path, meaning its distance from Earth changes. When a Full or New Moon coincides, or nearly coincides, with the point when the moon is closest to Earth, it's commonly known as a Super Moon. The technical term for this point in our planetary system is perigee-syzygy.

— ☾ —

Perigee refers to the point when the moon is closest to the Earth. A Full Moon in this position can appear up to 14 per cent bigger and 30 per cent brighter than a Full Moon at apogee – the most distant point from Earth. This is because more of the moon's reflected light from the sun reaches Earth.

For extra drama, try viewing the Super Moon close to the horizon as it rises or sets. Seeing the moon in comparison to trees and buildings on the panorama can exaggerate its appearance – creating what cynical scientists call the "moon illusion".

— ☾ —

The moon's effect on the tides is most significant at Full and New Moon when the gravitational power of the sun and moon combine. The extra gravitational pull of a Super Moon can boost this effect, but only by a matter of centimetres. These tides are called perigean spring tides or king tides.

— ☾ —

A Super Full Moon, or any Full Moon, is at its best at moonrise or moonset when the moon hugs the horizon – giving it a reflected orange or pink glow. Don't worry if you miss June 2022's Super Full Moon. There's another one in July 2022 – typically multiple Full Super Moons appear in consecutive months before the moon moves to a more distant point on its orbit.

MICRO MOON

June 2022 also features a Micro New Moon, meaning the New Moon coincides with the point in its orbit when it's furthermost away from Earth – or apogee.

— ☾ —

Like all New Moons, at first it will be completely invisible from Earth. When it does emerge, it will appear up to fourteen per cent smaller and thirty per cent dimmer than a dazzling Super Moon. This makes it a great time to stargaze; with no moonlight to wash out the stars, they can take centre stage.

We see the world piece by piece, as the sun, the moon, the animal, the tree; but the whole, of which these are shining parts, is the soul.

RALPH WALDO EMERSON

MOON SAYINGS FROM AROUND THE WORLD

The Spanish expression *quedarse a la luna de Valencia* – which is used to denote disappointment or being stranded – can be traced back to the Middle Ages when Valencia's old city walls were still standing. Legend has it that the city gates were locked at ten o'clock every night, and didn't open again until dawn. Latecomers who missed these gates were forced to spend the night under the Valencian Moon. According to another theory, latecomers spent the night on a crescent-shaped bench.

— ☾ —

The full phrase *quedarse a la luna de Valencia* is falling out of fashion. However, the shortened version *estar en la luna* is still used to mean absent-minded or daydreaming.

— ☾ —

The old Italian phrase *avere la luna di traverso* can be literally translated as "to have a sideways moon". It is still used to describe being in a bad mood. The phrase originates from the common belief that the moon had an influence on people's behaviour, even inciting confusion or excitement.

Être dans la lune is the French version of the English phrase "head in the clouds". It's used to describe someone who's daydreaming.

— ☾ —

The Portuguese use a similar phrase: *cabeça na lua* or "head on the moon", to describe someone who's distracted or forgetful.

— ☾ —

"The moon is always fuller on the other side", is the Cantonese equivalent of the English phrase "The grass is always greener on the other side."

— ☾ —

The Dutch phrase *loop naar de maan* literally means "walk to the moon". It's a Dutch way of telling someone to "take a hike" or go away. Belgian singer Yves Segers used the phrase as the title of his song from 2014.

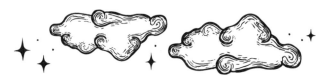

In the Basque region of Spain, *jenteek nahi lükee ekia ta argizagia junta ditean* means wishing the sun and the moon would merge. It's similar to the British phrase, "to have a finger in every pie".

— ☾ —

The Rutooro phrase *oli mumanzi nka kwezi* translates as "you're as brave as the moon".

— ☾ —

Mandarin has the phrase "the moon is dark, bright, round and missing a piece", which speaks of the uncertainty of life when all is not plain sailing.

— ☾ —

The German phrase *er lebt hinter dem Mond* meaning "he lives behind the moon", is used to describe someone who has no idea what's going on in the world.

— ☾ —

In Polish, the phrase *spaść z księżyca*, which translates as "to fall from the moon", is used to describe someone who is behaving strangely.

One moon shows in
every pool, in every
pool the one moon.

ZEN PROVERB

Chapter 7

July's Moon

Bask in the moonlight and
warm evening air throughout
this month. July 2022 brings
another Super Full Moon.

HERBS AND THUNDER

July's Wort Moon has roots in the Old English word for plants. Worts or wyrts were the Anglo Saxon name for medicinal plants or herbs. Used alongside charms, prayers, folklore and amulets, herbal remedies took pride of place in the Old English medicine cabinet. July – the height of the growing season – was a time to stock up from nature's apothecary. Another Anglo-Saxon moniker for this moon was the Hay Moon, after the July hay harvest.

— ☾ —

Native American Omaha and Northern Arapaho tribes referred to July's Full Moon as the Moon When Buffalos Bellow, after the sounds made by buffalos rutting at this time of year.

— ☾ —

Other names for this Full Moon include the Thunder Moon. In the Pacific Northwest of America, the Tlingit tribe called July's Full Moon the Salmon Moon, while the Anishaabe Tribe of the Great Lakes and Lake Winnipeg called it the Raspberry Moon.

July's Moon in Literature

Let's go to market in the moon,
And buy some dreams together,
Slip on your little silver shoon,
And don your cap and feather;
No need of petticoat or stocking –
No one up there will think it shocking.

Across the dew,
Just I and you,
With all the world behind us;
Away from rules,
Away from fools,
Where nobody can find us.

RICHARD LE GALLIENNE,
"MOON-MARKETING"

T'was noontide of summer,
And mid-time of night;
And stars, in their orbits,
Shone pale, thro' the light
Of the brighter, cold moon,
Mid planets her slaves,
Herself in the Heavens,
Her beam on the waves.
I gazed awhile
On her cold smile;
Too cold – too cold for me –
There pass'd, as a shroud,
A fleecy cloud,
And I turned away to thee,
Proud Evening Star,
In thy glory afar,
And dearer thy beam shall be;
For joy to my heart
Is the proud part
Thou bearest in Heaven at night,
And more I admire
Thy distant fire,
Than that colder, lowly light.

EDGAR ALLAN POE,
"EVENING STAR"

Come, heart, where hill is heaped upon hill:
For there the mystic brotherhood
Of sun and moon and hollow and wood
And river and stream work out their will.

W. B. YEATS,
FROM "INTO THE TWILIGHT"

— ☾ —

A moon-flooded prairie; a straying
Of leal-hearted lovers; a baying
Of far away watching dogs; a dreaming
Of brown-fisted farmers; a gleaming
Of fireflies eddying nigh, —
And that is July!

JAMES N. MATTHEWS,
FROM "JULY IN THE WEST"

GLOWING SKIN, SHINING HAIR AND GOOD FORTUNE

Yearning for glowing skin? A Turkish custom suggests that bathing in water that's been in contact with moonlight causes the skin to glow. But be sure not to swallow any; water touched by moonlight is believed to bring bad luck to drinkers.

— ☾ —

Brazilian folklore suggests that cutting your hair during a Crescent Moon encourages luxurious growth – book an appointment for the end of the month!

— ☾ —

A Celtic belief suggests that jingling silver coins or turning them in your pocket during a Full Moon promotes good luck.

Hay fever sufferers beware: according to an Austrian tradition, sneezing while looking at the New Moon brings bad luck.

— ☾ —

Superstitious Italians welcome in the New Moon with an incantation. With a coin in each hand, they chant: *Benvenuta, Luna, che mi porti fortuna* ("Welcome, Moon, and may you bring me good fortune").

— ☾ —

In China, new mothers traditionally spend a month recuperating after giving birth. A baby's first moon celebration – known as Moon Yut – is a time to introduce the new baby to friends and family members.

THE MOON AND THE TIDES

Most shorelines see two high tides and two low tides every 24 hours. These are caused by the gravitational force of the sun and moon on the Earth's water.

— ☾ —

As the Earth spins, the side facing the moon experiences a gravitational pull that causes the first high tide, or tidal bulge. The second tide arises because the Earth and the moon are rotating about a common centre of mass – the barycentre. When the Earth spins away from the moon, at this point centrifugal force is stronger than the moon's gravity, causing the water to bulge again.

— ☾ —

In the Bay of Fundy, Canada, the combined pull of the moon and the sun move the tide up to 16 metres (52 feet). This so-called "tidal range" is much smaller in other parts of the world, where it only varies by 1 metre (3 feet).

SPRING TIDES AND NEAP TIDES

Did you know that spring tides have nothing to do with the seasons? The name is used to describe the two highest tides of a lunar month – when the water springs forward.

— ☾ —

During a Full or New Moon, the sun, moon and Earth are aligned and all pulling the water in the same direction. This creates a spring tide.

— ☾ —

These effects are at their strongest during a Super Moon when a New Moon or Full Moon is also a Perigee Moon – a moon orbiting at its closest point to Earth. The resulting Super Moon has super gravitational effects, causing extra-large spring tides.

— ☾ —

Smaller tides, called neap tides, are formed seven days after a spring tide, when the Earth, sun and moon are at right angles to each other. This causes the water to be pulled in different directions. Neap tides happen during a Quarter or Three-Quarter Moon.

Don't tell me the moon is shining. Show me the glint of light on broken glass.

ANTON CHEKHOV

DAYLIGHT MOON

Did you know that the moon doesn't just come out at night? Actually, it can be seen during the day just as often.

— ☾ —

The moon's rise and set have nothing to do with our night or day – it's determined by the moon's orbit around Earth. The Full Moon phase, when the moon is 180 degrees away from the sun, coincides with sunset and sunrise, and the Moon reigns all night long. But at other times during the lunar cycle, the time of moonrise varies.

— ☾ —

During daylight hours, the sun's light is scattered by the Earth's atmosphere, drowning out all but the brightest stars. However, the bigger, more brilliant moon is often visible.

The best time to catch a moon during the day is a week either side of the Full Moon. Before the Full Moon, the First Quarter Moon rises at noon in the east, and sets at midnight. Look out for it in the afternoon. After the Full Moon, the Third Quarter Moon rises at midnight and sets at noon in the west. Your best chance of seeing it is in the morning. At these points, the moon is often illuminated enough to be visible.

— ☾ —

During other phases, the moon is more difficult to spot during the day, due to its position relative to the sun. The closer the moon is to the sun, the more likely its reflected light will get lost in the sun's glare. At the time of a New Moon, the slim crescent is very close to the sun. It's almost invisible, but worth hunting out.

MEN ON THE MOON

On 19 July 1969, after travelling 240,000 miles (386,000 kilometres) in 76 hours as part of NASA's Apollo program, Apollo 11 entered into a lunar orbit. The following day, the lunar module Eagle, manned by Neil Armstrong and Buzz Aldrin, landed on the southwestern edge of the moon's Sea of Tranquillity. Speaking to Mission Control in Houston, Texas, Armstrong confirmed: "The Eagle has landed." Hours later, the men took the first steps by humans on another planetary body. At the crucial moment when Armstrong stepped out of the craft, his now-famous words were slightly garbled by his microphone. He was quoted as saying: "That's one small step for man, one giant leap for mankind." He later confirmed he'd actually said: "That's one small step for a man, one giant leap for mankind", which makes more sense.

— ☾ —

A total of 12 people have walked on the moon including Armstrong and Aldrin. The Apollo programme continued until 1972, landing a further five missions. These missions have enabled astronauts to conduct experiments, collect samples, explore the lunar landscape and even play golf.

Chapter 8

August's Moon

Settle a feud under a Full Moon
this month – and marvel at
the rare Blue Moon if you're
fortunate enough to see it.

GREEN CORN AND QUARRELS

Known as the Grain Moon or the Green Corn Moon in Britain, August's moon has always been tied to the season's first harvest.

— ☾ —

The Full Moon this month often coincided with jubilant Lammas festivals. This annual gathering celebrated the first harvest of the year. It was also a time when flare-ups between farmers and commoners over grazing rights on common land played out. These rights allowed commoners to graze their livestock, gather firewood and cut turf from common land following the hay harvest, between Lammas Day (1 August) and 6 April. These stormy affairs led August's Moon to be called the Dispute Moon.

— ☾ —

Another moniker for August's Full Moon is the Red Moon, due to the reddish complexion it often takes on in the summer haze.

Both Algonquian-speaking tribes and colonists in North America nicknamed August's Full Moon the Sturgeon Moon, thanks to the many sturgeon pods that were found in the Great Lakes of Huron, Michigan, Erie, Ontario and Superior at this time of year.

— ☽ —

Other Native American tribes named August's Full Moon after nature that was bountiful on their patch at this time of year: the Blackberry Moon, the Flying Up Moon – after fledgling birds – and the Salmon Moon.

— ☽ —

Colonial Americans sometimes called this moon the Dog Days Moon. The phrase "dog days" (the hottest days of the year in July and August) actually originated with the ancient Greeks and Romans, who noticed the bright dog star, Sirius, appears near the sun at this time of year. The dawn rising of Sirius was blamed for the heat and humidity of the season.

When you see the setting, wait for the rising. Why worry about a sunset or a fading moon?

RUMI

✦ *Did you know?* ✦

August's New Moon marked the beginning of a period of thanks and celebration for ancient Egyptians. Farmers noticed the first glimmer of Sirius on the eastern horizon before sunrise often tallied with the annual flooding of the Nile. These welcome floodwaters – called the inundation – enriched the soil, helping farmers grow crops on their parched land. As such, Sirius became the farmers' "watchdog", and the August New Moon kicked off a period of thanks and celebration.

The August Full Moon also heralds the Hindu festival of Raksha Bandhan, which celebrates sibling bonds.

The Buddhist holiday of Nikini Poya, after the first Buddhist council that formed over 2,400 years ago, also takes place under August's Full Moon.

August's Moon
in Literature

"Far away beyond the pine-woods", he
answered, in a low dreamy voice, "there is
a little garden. There the grass grows long
and deep, there are the great white stars of
the hemlock flower, there the nightingale
sings all night long. All night long he sings,
and the cold, crystal moon looks down, and
the yew-tree spreads out its giant arms over
the sleepers."

OSCAR WILDE,
FROM *THE CANTERVILLE GHOST*

She had forgotten how the August night
Was level as a lake beneath the moon,
In which she swam a little, losing sight
Of shore; and how the boy, that was at noon
Simple enough, not different from the rest,
Wore now a pleasant mystery as he went,
Which seemed to her an honest enough test
Whether she loved him, and she
　was content.
So loud, so loud the million crickets' choir...
So sweet the night, so long-drawn-out
　and late...
And if the man were not her spirit's mate,
Why was her body sluggish with desire?
Stark on the open field the moonlight fell,
But the oak tree's shadow was deep and
　black and secret as a well.

EDNA ST VINCENT MILLAY,
"SHE HAD FORGOTTEN HOW
THE AUGUST NIGHT"

It was upon a Lammas night,
When corn rigs are bonnie,
Beneath the moon's unclouded light,
I held awa to Annie.

ROBERT BURNS,
FROM "THE RIGS O' BARLEY"

Bide by the Moon
follow Her glow
By the light of the New
we renew and grow
By the Waxing Quarter
our determination shows
By the Full Moon's light
our desires we know
By the Waning Quarter
we ebb after flow
By the Dark Moon's presence
we return what we've sown
Bide by the Moon
follow Her glow.

ANONYMOUS,
"BIDE BY THE MOON"

BLUE MOONS

The term "Blue Moon" has been part of the English language for hundreds of years. However today's definition of a Blue Moon – when a second Full Moon sneaks into a single calendar month – has only been used since 1946. Historically, the term was used for a similar phenomenon: the third or fourth Full Moon appearing during a season of three months.

— ☾ —

While these calendar events are rare, incidents when the moon actually appears blue are even more out of the ordinary. However, very occasionally, when the Earth's atmosphere holds enough large dust or smoke particles to diffract red light, the moon can look blue from Earth.

In 1883, the Indonesian volcano Krakatoa exploded, sending enough dust into the atmosphere to tint the Earth's sunsets green and the moon blue for nearly two years. Likewise, in 1927, when late Indian monsoons led to an extra-long dry season, the resulting dust gave the moon a blue hue. A massive forest fire in western Canada in 1951 had the same effect.

— ☾ —

All these anomalies have led to the phrase "once in a blue moon" being used to describe rare events.

BLACK MOONS

The definition of a Black Moon is even hazier. The most common definition of a Black Moon is the flip side of a Blue Moon: a month with two New Moons. By another definition, when a season has four New Moons, the third is called a Black Moon.

— ☾ —

Because February is only 28 days long – shorter than a lunar month – once every 19 years this month sees no New Moon. Likewise, once every nineteen years there's no Full Moon in February. This is sometimes called a Black Moon.

— ☾ —

Black Moons hold special significance for some Pagans, who believe spells cast in their darkness become more potent.

The moon is a friend for

the lonesome to talk to.

CARL SANDBURG

ABUNDANCE, ROMANCE AND BETRAYAL

According to one Welsh adage, if a relative dies during a Blue Moon, three more family members will suffer the same fate.

— ☾ —

Another superstition claims that looking at a Blue Moon through glass brings bad luck for 30 days.

— ☾ —

Picking flowers and gathering berries during a Blue Moon is said to bring abundance, love and beauty into your life.

— ☾ —

The moon has long associations with pregnancy: many cultures believe women are more fertile during a Blue Moon.

— ☾ —

Goal setting beneath a Blue Moon is said to make dreams come true soon afterwards.

Turning down the covers on your bed during a Blue Moon makes women more fertile according to an Old English tradition.

— ☾ —

Watch your back during a Blue Moon. Some say the name comes from the Old English word *belewe* for blue, which means "to betray".

— ☾ —

Need some good luck? Next time you see a Blue Moon, turn over a coin in your pocket for good fortune in all aspects of life.

— ☾ —

In years gone by, gangsters believed robberies attempted on the third day of a Blue Moon were destined to fail.

— ☾ —

Stubborn wart? Try the old remedy of blowing on it nine times while the Blue Moon is full.

Chapter 9

September's Moon

Admire this month's Harvest
Moon: the Full Moon closest
to the Autumn Equinox.

HARVEST, SONGS AND HONEY

When September's Full Moon is the nearest moon to the Autumn Equinox in the Northern hemisphere, it earns the title Harvest Moon.

— ☾ —

Other monikers include the Corn Moon, the Fruit Moon or the Barley Moon, after the crops that are gathered during this season. Celtic farmers often sang songs to spur workers along and celebrate their harvest. Shakespeare's *The Tempest* includes tales of singing in the fields, including a "Reapers Dance". *The Golden Bough*, first published in 1890, describes English harvesters decorating the last sheaf of grain with ribbons and flowers while others sang.

— ☾ —

For some Buddhists in Bangladesh and Thailand, September's Full Moon is called Modhu Purnima – the Honey Full Moon. It's tied to a honey-offering festival that remembers an elephant and a monkey who fed Buddha fruit and honey, bringing peace between two factions.

WHAT'S SO SPECIAL ABOUT
THE HARVEST MOON?

As the moon travels through its lunar phases, the time of moonrise changes – getting later by around 50 minutes each day. Typically, a Full Moon rises approximately 50 minutes after sunset and stays in the sky all night. At this point in the lunar cycle, the moon is directly opposite the sun. This means it only rises above the horizon when the sun sinks out of view.

— ☾ —

The Harvest Moon has special astronomical significance because, for a few nights, it rises earlier than most Full Moons – less than 50 minutes later than the day before. At this time of year, in the Northern hemisphere, the moon's eastward orbital motion is moving further north. For skywatchers in the Northern hemisphere, the further north an object appears, the longer its arc across the sky, and the longer it's visible above the horizon. This shortens the time between sunset and moonrise.

In the days before tractor lights, the lamp of the Harvest Moon illuminated farmers' fields immediately after sunset and through the evening for several nights in a row. This gifted them an extra few hours to gather their crops.

— ☾ —

The Harvest Moon can appear bigger and brighter and more orange than other moons. This is an optical illusion. The moon looks larger and redder when it's close to the horizon because it's being seen in comparison to other objects such as trees and buildings on the skyline. It's also being seen through the Earth's atmosphere, which absorbs blue light and reflects red light.

MOONCAKES AND TOGETHERNESS

September often sees the Chinese celebrating their Mid-Autumn Festival. This custom dates back over 3,000 years. It's a time for families to come together, eat Mooncakes and contemplate the bright Full Moon, which symbolizes togetherness and reunion in Chinese culture.

— ☾ —

The Japanese celebrate a variation of this festival with their own Tsukimi festival. People gather to view the Full Moon, pray for a good harvest and offer seasonal produce. Traditional treats include rice dumplings and sweet potato, giving rise to the name Potato Harvest Moon in some parts of Japan.

September's Moon in Literature

Under the harvest moon,
When the soft silver
Drips shimmering
Over the garden nights,
Death, the gray mocker,
Comes and whispers to you
As a beautiful friend
Who remembers.

Under the summer roses
When the flagrant crimson
Lurks in the dusk
Of the wild red leaves,
Love, with little hands,
Comes and touches you
With a thousand memories,
And asks you
Beautiful, unanswerable questions.

CARL SANDBURG,
"UNDER THE HARVEST MOON"

At the top of the house the apples are laid
  in rows,
And the skylight lets the moonlight in, and those
Apples are deep-sea apples of green. There goes
A cloud on the moon in the autumn night.

A mouse in the wainscot scratches, and
  scratches, and then
There is no sound at the top of the house of men
Or mice; and the cloud is blown, and the
  moon again
Dapples the apples with deep-sea light.

They are lying in rows there, under the
  gloomy beams;
On the sagging floor; they gather the
  silver streams
Out of the moon, those moonlit apples
  of dreams,
And quiet is the steep stair under.

In the corridors under there is nothing but sleep.
And stiller than ever on orchard boughs
  they keep
Tryst with the moon, and deep is the
  silence, deep
On moon-washed apples of wonder.

JOHN DRINKWATER,
"MOONLIT APPLES"

FLOODS, MISTS AND BLACKBERRIES

Michaelmas on 29 September – or the Christian Feast of Michael and All Angels – is one of the four quarter-days in England. These days mark the beginning of each quarter of the year. The age of the moon on Michaelmas has also been used to predict floods, with an old proverb stating: "So many days old the moon is on Michaelmas day, so many floods after."

— ☾ —

If you're making sloe gin this month, be sure to only pick berries during a Full Moon. In Irish folklore, the Blackthorn is the home of unfriendly Lunantisidhe, or moon fairies, who curse those who disturb them. During the Full Moon they leave the bush to worship the moon goddess, so it's the safest time to harvest sloe berries.

— ☾ —

In the 1670 publication *The Shepherd of Banbury's Rules to Judge the Changes of the Weather*, the misty moon is used to predict the weather in the following rules:

A general mist before the Sun rises,
near the Full Moon — fair weather.

If mists in the New Moon — rain
in the Old [Moon].

If mists in the Old [Moon] — rain
in the New Moon.

DON'T LOOK NOW!

The Hindu festival of Ganesh Chaturthi often falls in September. The festival celebrates the birth of Lord Ganesha, the beloved Hindu elephant-headed God. Worshipped for his ability to remove obstacles and bring good fortune, his life represents fortune, prosperity and wisdom. But why is it unlucky to look at the moon during this festival? According to Hindu Mythology, Lord Ganesha was riding his mouse after a big night out when he fell over. Embarrassing! He was made to feel even more awkward by the moon god, Chandra, who laughed at him in an early version of body shaming. The angry Ganesha cursed the moon and took away his shine. The moon eventually talked him around, but to this day it's considered a bad omen to look at the moon during Ganesh Chaturthi – anyone doing so will face false allegations.

LUNAR LOGIC TO LIVE BY

Feeling rushed? Slow down with
the Ghanaian Proverb:

*"The moon moves slowly, but it
gets across the town."*

Find contentment with the Spanish proverb:

"If you have the moon, ignore the stars."

Feel free to change your mind
with the German proverb:

*"Promises are like the Full Moon:
they diminish day by day."*

Take strength from a Chinese
proverb about patience:

*"Keep watch until the clouds part,
and you'll see moonlight."*

Feeling righteous? Remember the
Native American proverb:

*"Don't judge a man until you have walked
two moons in his moccasins."*

Learn to be yourself with the Czech proverb:

*"The moon does not care
if the dog barks at it.*

The moon is a silver

pin-head vast,

That holds the heaven's

tent-hangings fast.

WILLIAM R. ALGER

MOON DESERT

The moon is around 100 times drier than the Sahara Desert. With no protective atmosphere, the extreme climate of scorching days and freezing nights means any evaporated water quickly disappears into space. Previously, scientists have detected lunar ice in the permanently shadowed craters around the moon's poles. Studies have also found faint traces of water on the moon's sunlit areas. Researchers still need to understand more about these watery discoveries to determine how significant they could be in future missions. The possibility that the water could be used in future missions both as a resource for scientific purposes and by astronauts makes the exploration all the more exciting.

MOON SIGNS

While most people know their star sign – or sun sign – many are unaware that the moon also plays a starring role in astrology.

— ☾ —

The position of the sun at a person's time of birth determines their star sign. The Earth spends roughly 30 to 31 days in each sign as it orbits around the sun. Therefore, sun signs are shared by everyone born within a monthly timeframe. Astrologers believe sun signs determine only the rough brushstrokes of a person's characteristics – their ego, their drive and their outward persona.

— ☾ —

Moon signs however, are more individual. They're calculated using a person's exact time and place of birth, which determines the position of the moon – the moon only stays in each sign for around two days. As such, astrologers maintain that moon signs reveal more about the intimate aspects of a person's character – their emotions, sensitivities and their private inner world. This influence may explain why people of the same star sign can have very different personalities.

For astrologers, a moon in a fire sign (Aries, Leo, Sagittarius) creates a tendency for dramatic emotional reactions, whereas a moon in an Earth sign (Capricorn, Taurus, Virgo) makes for a stable, grounded person. Those with their moon in a water sign (Cancer, Pisces, Scorpio) tend to have deep-running emotions. A moon in an air sign (Aquarius, Gemini, Libra) drives individuals to approach emotional situations in a detached and intellectual way.

— ☾ —

Calculating your moon sign relies on knowing your exact time of birth. Professional astrologers can help, or calculators are available online.

— ☾ —

Astrologers believe that understanding your moon sign can help make sense of how you behave when you're vulnerable, the kind of parent you're likely to be and how you relate within sentimental and intimate relationships. They also believe that knowing your moon sign can help you understand what makes you feel most comfortable and safe. So, move over star signs, when it comes to self-knowledge the moon is where it's at!

Chapter 10

October's Moon

An eclipse is a rare treat for any moon watcher. In 2021, October's moon will partially cover the sun for approximately one hour and 43 minutes.

HUNTERS AND NEW PASTURES

The Hunter's Moon is so-called because October was the preferred month to hunt deer and foxes, which were fat after the summer and unable to take cover in the ploughed fields.

— ☾ —

Like the Harvest Moon, the Hunter's Moon is also an early riser, giving hunters a hand to stalk their prey in the early hours.

— ☾ —

Another name for October's Moon is the Travel Moon, perhaps due to the migration of birds at this time of year, or because tribes left their summer hunting grounds and travelled to shelter during this month.

MAIDEN, MOTHER AND CRONE: THE MOON IN FEMALE ARCHETYPES

Pagans, Wiccans and neopagans honour life's passage through a threefold goddess called the Triple Goddess. Her individual aspects, known as the Maiden, the Mother and the Crone, are aligned with the heavens, in the phases of the moon, and with earth in the seasons and in the human life cycle.

— ☾ —

While women progress through these phases in a literal and linear sense during the course of their lifetimes, each aspect of the Triple Goddess has universal qualities that will resonate with everyone. Indeed, the Triple Goddess could be said to reflect the complexities of the human experience, as well as the universal flow of birth, life and death or transformation.

The Maiden is represented by the waxing moon and embodies birth, inspiration, growth, creativity, curiosity and play. Her optimism, excitement and energy can be felt literally in youth, but also in the spark of a new idea, at the beginning of a new chapter or in playful moments and simple pleasures.

— ☾ —

The Mother is represented by the full moon and embodies nourishment and realization. Her energy is channelled with the birth of a child, which triggers the instincts of unconditional love, protection and responsibility. Self-discipline, patience and resourcefulness are also characteristics of this phase. The energy of the mother is not limited to motherhood, it can also show up when caring for others or nurturing a project or relationship.

— ☾ —

The Crone is represented by the waning moon and embodies maturity, endings and transformation. Her energy is wise, intuitive and masterful. The Crone is empowered to speak out, and is anything but a people pleaser. She is undaunted by change; in fact she knows that endings also bring new beginnings. Literally, women enter this phase with the menopause or when children fly the nest, but Crone energies can also be felt in sharp observations born from experience or intuition, when lessons are learned and when relationships or projects end.

— ☾ —

While the neopagan Triple Goddess is a twentieth-century concept first described by the author and poet Robert Graves, in his book *The White Goddess: a Historical Grammar of Poetic Myth*, many historical antecedents to the goddess exist: the late fourth-century and early fifth-century grammarian, Servius, described a goddess who was at-once called Lucina, Diana and Hecate, because she was assigned with the powers of birth, growth and death. These three powers inspired worshippers to see her as a threefold form. Temples were built where three roads met in her honour. Servius's text included drawings of a Crescent Moon, a Half Moon and a Full Moon.

October's Moon in Literature

When I gaze at the Moon
All things seem sad
Though I know the Autumn
Comes not to me alone.

ŌE NO **CHISATO**
"POEM 23"

The Hunter's Moon rides high,
High o'er the close-cropped plain;
Across the desert sky
The herded clouds amain
Scamper tumultuously,
Chased by the hounding wind
That yelps behind.

The clamorous hunt is done,
Warm-housed the kennelled pack;
One huntsman rides alone
With dangling bridle slack;
He wakes a hollow tone,
Far echoing to his horn
In clefts forlorn.

The Hunter's Moon rides low,
Her course is nearly sped.
Where is the panting roe?
Where hath the wild deer fled?
Hunter and hunted now
Lie in oblivion deep:
Dead or asleep.

MATHILDE BLIND,
"THE HUNTER'S MOON"

The owl is abroad, the bat, the toad,
And so is the cat-a-mountain;
The ant and the mole sit both in a hole;
And frog peeps out o' the fountain;
The dogs they bay, and the
    timbrels play;
The spindle is now a-turning;
The moon it is red, and the stars
    are fled;
But all the sky is a-burning.

BEN JONSON,
FROM "THE WITCHES' SONG"

DECAPITATED DEMONS, SKY WOLVES AND CELESTIAL DRAGONS

In ancient times terrifying beasts were often blamed for eating the sun during a solar eclipse. No wonder the earliest word for an eclipse in Chinese is *shih*, which means "to eat".

— ☾ —

In ancient China, the sun was gobbled by a celestial dragon during an eclipse. In Norse mythology, two wolf-like creatures were believed to have swallowed the star. Indian mythology tells the story of a decapitated head of a cunning demon biting the sun. In Armenian folklore, a dragon does the eating, while in Vietnam, the sun is ravaged by a giant frog. For the Pomo, an indigenous tribe from Northwestern USA, the sun is said to be consumed by an angry bear.

— ☾ —

The word "eclipse" originates from the Greek word *Ekleípō* meaning "abandonment", which reveals how ancient Greeks felt when their sun god, Helios, disappeared during an eclipse.

This feeling is echoed in Transylvanian folklore, where stories of an angry sun turning away from the sins of the world abound.

— ☾ —

The Native American Tewa tribe also felt abandoned, believing an eclipse meant the angry sun was returning to his home in the underworld.

— ☾ —

Rulers through history saw eclipses as harbingers of their downfall. When King Henry I died following a solar eclipse in 1133, many courtiers put it down to the celestial phenomenon.

— ☾ —

Terrified Chippewa people fired flaming arrows into the sky, trying to rekindle the sun during an eclipse. Tribes in Peru did the same in an attempt to ward off an attacking beast.

— ☾ —

Native people in Colombia yelled promises at the darkening sky, vowing to work hard and mend their ways.

Traditional stories about fierce beasts during an eclipse led some ancient cultures to believe pregnant women and their unborn babies were also at risk. Mexican superstitions warned that if a pregnant woman views an eclipse, her unborn child is at risk of cleft palate, birthmarks or blindness.

✦ *Did you know?* ✦

Not everyone feared eclipses. Some cultures saw them in a romantic light. In German mythology, the female sun and the male moon had a happy marriage: an eclipse was them coming together for companionship.

People of ancient Benin, in West Africa, believed eclipses occurred to give a rare moment of privacy to the sun and the moon.

In one Tahitian myth, the sun and moon are lovers coming together, causing an eclipse. Lost in the moment, they lit stars to ease their return.

Eclipses weren't feared by Bohemian miners as they believed gold was more accessible at this time.

For the Native American Navajo culture, an eclipse – and the rebirth of the sun – was a time for introspection, renewal and transformation.

MIST, WIND AND
FALLING TEMPERATURES

The "eclipse wind" had baffled scientists since it was first noted by Edmund Halley of Halley's Comet fame. This strange weather phenomenon creates falling temperatures, a change in wind conditions and mist during a solar eclipse.

— ☾ —

Halley noted that the "chill and damp which attended the darkness" caused "some sense of horror" among the spectators during the eclipse of 1715.

— ☾ —

For many, the fog or dew caused by an eclipse was considered dangerous. The Japanese covered their wells, believing poison would drop from the sky. Alaskan natives thought the moisture and dew could cause sickness; crockery and utensils were turned upside down and washed.

The presence of an "eclipse wind" remained in debate until the partial eclipse on 20 March 2015. During this eclipse, an army of 4,500 citizen scientists around the UK, led by Dr Luke Barnard and Meteorologists at the University of Reading, conducted a National Eclipse Weather Experiment. Their findings – with further analysis from Professor Giles Harrison and Professor Suzanne Gray – revealed the cause of the eclipse wind.

They discovered that as the sun disappears behind the moon, the ground suddenly cools and warm air stops rising. Shifts in this "boundary layer", which divides high-level winds from those at ground level, cause a drop in wind speed and a change in its direction, much like at sunset.

What's in a name?

According to the International Astronomical Union (IAU), a natural satellite cannot be both a moon and a planet, but, as we know, our moon is not classed a planet. However, it does have lots of planet-like qualities.

Like the Earth, the moon is made up of three layers: a crust, a mantel and a central core. This means the moon was formed in the same way as a planet.

— ☽ —

Like the Earth, the moon has active geology. The Apollo missions picked up thousands of "moonquakes", which revealed the surface was still evolving.

— ☽ —

Like Earth, the moon's evolution was influenced by active lava-spewing volcanoes. The dark pitted marks on its surface are old lava flows. Samples gathered on the Apollo missions contained volcanic glass caused by fiery explosions that are believed to have died out around three billion years ago.

— ☽ —

These planet-like qualities mean the status of the moon is up for debate, and the IAU has been known to change its mind about the definition of planets in the past. (In 2006, they reclassified Pluto as a dwarf planet.) Moon-gazers keen to keep tabs on the status of the moon should watch this space!

It dawned upon me up
there in the moon as a
thing I ought always to
have known, that man is
not made simply to go about
being safe and comfortable
and well fed and amused.

H. G. WELLS

Chapter 11

November's Moon

November's moon is an ideal
time to hunker down and
reflect on the year so far.

FROST AND BEAVERS

The chilling sight of the Beaver Moon in the November sky was an annual reminder for Native American tribes to set beaver traps in their rivers before the water froze over.

Beaver fur was vital for survival in harsh North American winters. Native American tribes, such as the Cree, Arapaho and Abenaki tribes, called November's Full Moon the Moon When Rivers Start to Freeze for similar reasons.

As the last moon before the Winter Solstice, for Pagans, November's moon is dubbed the Mourning Moon. Quiet reflection, cleansing and letting go of the year's worries in time for a fresh start in the New Year are encouraged.

For the Celts, the moon following Samhain – the Celtic New Year, or Halloween – was connected to death and the afterlife. Believing water was a gateway to the underworld, they called November's moon the Reed Moon after the reeds growing in pools and rivers. The haunting sound of reed instruments was connected to rites for the dead and was thought to resemble calls from the other side.

Escape from the black

cloud that surrounds you.

Then you will see your

own light as radiant

as the Full Moon.

RUMI

FESTIVALS OF LIGHT

In Thailand, the Loy Krathong festival usually falls in November. In the twelfth month of the Thai lunar calendar, festival-goers create tiny lotus-shaped rafts decorated with candles, incense and flowers. On the night of the Full Moon, they launch these into rivers, canals and ponds while making a wish.

— ☾ —

The Diwali festival – also known as Deepavali, Dipavali, Dewali, Deepawali, or the Festival of Lights – is celebrated in October or November each year. The chosen date has important astrological significance: beginning just before the New Moon, it marks the new lunar year and the season's harvest. The planetary positions are believed to be favourable at this time, bringing wealth and prosperity to all. Diwali is a Sanskrit a word that translates as "garland of lamps". Hindus, Sikhs, Buddhists and Jains all celebrate the victory of good over evil by lighting oil lamps, candles and fireworks.

November's Moon in Literature

No sun – no moon!
No morn – no noon –
No dawn – no dusk – no proper time
    of day.

No warmth, no cheerfulness, no healthful
    ease,
No comfortable feel in any member –
No shade, no shine, no butterflies, no bees,
No fruits, no flowers, no leaves, no birds! –
November!

THOMAS HOOD,
"NOVEMBER"

The moon has a face like the clock in the hall;
She shines on thieves on the garden wall,
On streets and fields and harbour quays,
And birdies asleep in the forks of the trees.

The squalling cat and the squeaking mouse,
The howling dog by the door of the house,
The bat that lies in bed at noon,
All love to be out by the light of the Moon.

But all of the things that belong to the day
Cuddle to sleep to be out of her way;
And flowers and children close their eyes
Till up in the morning the sun shall arise.

ROBERT LOUIS STEVENSON,
"THE MOON"

Pity me not because the light of day
At close of day no longer walks the sky;
Pity me not for beauties passed away
From field and thicket as the year
  goes by;
Pity me not the waning of the moon,
Nor that the ebbing tide goes out to sea,
Nor that a man's desire is hushed
  so soon,
And you no longer look with love on me.
This have I known always: Love is
  no more
Than the wide blossom which the
  wind assails,
Than the great tide that treads the
  shifting shore.
Strewing fresh wreckage gathered in
  the gales;
Pity me that the heart is slow to learn.

EDNA ST VINCENT MILLAY,
"PITY ME NOT BECAUSE
THE LIGHT OF DAY"

MOON WORDS AND IDIOMS

Living among over 96,000 lakes has inspired the Swedes to come up with a word to capture the trail of moonlight on water. *Mångata* combines the word *måne*, for moon, and *gata*, meaning street, to describe this unique beauty.

The word *gümüşservi* in Turkish refers to the same phenomenon, though its literal translation – silver cypress tree – is more abstract.

In English, to be "over the moon" is to be extremely happy. The phrase dates back at least 500 years, to the traditional nursery rhyme, "Hey diddle diddle, the cat and the fiddle, the cow jumped over the moon..."

Saying "many moons" to describe a long time uses the word moon in its early sense, when it was used in place of the word "month". Indeed, the etymology of the two words are similar. The Old English words for moon, *mōna* and month, *mōnath*, have Germanic origin and are related to Dutch *maan* and German *mond*. All have an Indo-European root shared by the Latin *mensis* for month, and *metiri* for measure – because the moon was used to measure time. They're also related to the Greek *mēn* for month.

— ☾ —

The phrases "ask for the moon", "promise the moon" and "shoot for the moon", use the moon as a symbol of the impossible.

— ☾ —

To do a "moonlight flit" is to suddenly vanish under the cover of darkness.

Moonshine is a clear liquor with murky origins: it was first used in the 1811 publication Dictionary of the Vulgar Tongue, by Francis Grose to describe illegal alcohol smuggled off the coasts of Kent and Sussex by night in eighteenth-century England. The phrase cropped up again during prohibition in the USA when illicit liquor was produced and smuggled under the cover of darkness. Contemporary versions of this now legal drink retain its dangerous reputation.

To "moon" about something or someone is to mope or be sad.

The purpose of life is the investigation of the sun, the moon and the heavens.

ANAXAGORAS

THE MOON AND THE
MENSTRUAL CYCLE

The lunar cycle is around the same length as the menstrual cycle. Similarly, just as the moon cycles through phases, female hormones and fertility also wax and wane.

— ☾ —

Ancient cultures and early scientists linked the menstrual cycle and fertility to the moon. In Incan mythology and religion, Mama Quilla – the goddess of the moon – was also the goddess of marriage and the menstrual cycle.

— ☾ —

For precolonial Māori, the moon was said to be the "true husband" of all women, and menstrual blood was seen as holy and powerful.

— ☾ —

For the ancient Chinese, the moon was associated with water and connected to a woman's "monthly water".

Charles Darwin advocated the idea that menstruation is linked to lunar activity, believing the 28-day menstrual cycle was evidence that our ancestors lived on the seashore in synchronicity with the tides.

— ☾ —

Even the word menstruation is related to moon. It comes from the Latin word for a month – *menses* – which in turn connects to the Greek word for moon, *mene*.

— ☾ —

But what about modern science? A study looking at a link between menstrual and lunar cycles in 1979 determined that a third of the 305 women studied had a cycle the same length as the lunar cycle. Almost two-thirds started their cycle in the lighter half of the lunar cycle. Another study in 1986 confirmed a synchronous relationship between the menstrual cycle and lunar rhythms.

— ☾ —

More recent studies refute the idea, but many women still find comfort and empowerment in relating their monthly cycle to the cycle of the moon.

Author Miranda Gray felt inspired to delve deeper after reading *The Wise Wound* by Penelope Shuttle and Peter Redgrove. "In it they referenced research that shows that women's ovulation and menstruation tend to oscillate around the times of the Full Moon or the Dark Moon," Miranda explained. "However, what was missing from their work was the female spiritual experience behind this 'revelation', and how it could have influenced earlier societies. From my own personal observations and the observations of other women, it seemed that our beliefs, thoughts, expectations, goals, and needs in life affect the orientation of our cycles between the 'Red Moon Cycle' or the 'White Moon Cycle' – titles that I first introduced in my own book on the subject: *Red Moon*."

Gray describes two main patterns of menstruation; "White Moon" bleeding and "Red Moon" bleeding, and women will attune to both patterns during different points in their lives, depending on which serves them best.

A White Moon Cycle – the most common cycle – involves bleeding with the New Moon and ovulating with the Full Moon. A Red Moon Cycle sees a woman bleeding with the Full Moon and becoming fertile during the New Moon. The energies of a woman following a White Moon Cycle are focused outwards, with an emphasis on fertility, external creativity and motherhood. This creativity could be in the form of a potential pregnancy or expressed in the world by creating something personal. Women following this orientation of their cycle can feel a surge in intuition during their period, with an urge to rest and recuperate, ready to create new life during the next phrase.

On the flip side, a woman following a Red Moon Cycle can feel she is channelling her creativity inwards. Rather than creating a baby, her energies can be more focused on self-actualization, spirituality, and empowering other women – think shamans, healers, wisdom keepers and witches. Red Moon Cycle women benefit from ovulatory energy, while other women are bleeding. Likewise, while other women are ovulating, the intuitive menstrual powers of Red Moon Cycle women are at their height. They are able to take care of those busy with procreation and use their gifts to bring about magic, art and healing.

ATTUNING TO MOON CYCLES

Today's women may find themselves out of sorts due to modern lifestyles that stifle natural rhythms. However, help is at hand for those interested in attuning to a particular moon cycle. It's all about harnessing the biological effect of natural moonlight.

— ☾ —

The first step is to align your circadian (sleep) rhythm to the cycle of the moon: embracing natural sunlight during the day and retreating to darkness during the night. Darkness is especially important when the moon is new or waning. It may sound simple, but sunglasses, smartphones, changing shift patterns, jet lag and weekend lie-ins can all play havoc with natural rhythms.

— ☾ —

Embracing the power of natural moonlight – or at least replicating it – is also said to help. Turning on a 100-watt light bulb while you sleep during the five to six days of the Full Moon and sleeping in complete darkness for the rest of the month has been shown to regulate menstruation. Or why not sleep under the stars during the next Full Moon?

Chapter 12

December's Moon

The long nights of December
are a good time to connect to a
Full Moon that shines above the
horizon for a long period of time
in the Northern hemisphere.

LONG NIGHTS AND OAK

The Old English Anglo-Saxon name for December's Full Moon is the Moon Before Yule, after the old Northern European winter festival of the same name.

— ☾ —

Commonly, December's moon is also called the Cold Moon in the Northern hemisphere. The name has Native American roots.

— ☾ —

Other names include the Oak Moon – a reference to ancient druid practices observed by the Romans. The Roman historian Pliny the Elder recorded harvesting mistletoe from oak trees in the first century CE.

— ☾ —

The moniker Long Night Moon is a nod to the Winter Solstice in the Northern hemisphere and the shortest day of the year.

We are all like the bright moon, we still have our darker side.

KAHLIL GIBRAN

December's Moon in Literature

Therefore the moon, the governess
  of floods,
Pale in her anger, washes all the air,
That rheumatic diseases do abound:
And through this distemperature we see
The seasons alter.

WILLIAM SHAKESPEARE,
FROM *A MIDSUMMER NIGHT'S DREAM*

This Advent moon shines cold and clear,
These Advent nights are long;
Our lamps have burned year after year,
And still their flame is strong.
"Watchman, what of the night?" we cry,
Heart-sick with hope deferred:
"No speaking signs are in the sky,"
Is still the watchman's word.

CHRISTINA ROSSETTI,
FROM "ADVENT"

And now cold Earth was Arctic sea,
Each breath came dagger keen,
Two bergs of glinting ice were we,
The broad Moon sailed between;
There swam the mermaids, tailed
    and finned,
And Love went by upon the wind
As though it had not been.

ROBERT GRAVES,
FROM "FULL MOON"

Two statesmen met by moonlight.
Their ease was partly feigned.
They glanced about the prairie.
Their faces were constrained.
In various ways aforetime
They had misled the state,
Yet did it so politely
Their henchmen thought them great.
They sat beneath a hedge and spake
No word, but had a smoke.
A satchel passed from hand to hand.
Next day, the deadlock broke.

VACHEL LINDSAY,
"WHAT THE MOON SAW"

FROST AND PLENTIFUL HARVESTS

An Old English superstition claims that if Christmas falls on the day of a Dark Moon, the next year's harvest will be plentiful.

— ☾ —

In some parts of ancient Britain, a waxing moon at Christmas foretold a good harvest in the coming season. A waning moon indicated a lower yield.

— ☾ —

An old Scottish proverbs states: "If Winter's New Moon has horns sharp and defined, expect frost."

— ☾ —

According to Romany weather lore, "A small, high, cold, silver moon means frost."

— ☾ —

The Husband-man's Practice, published by J.M. in 1685, states: "When Christmas day cometh while the moon waxeth, it shall be a very good year, and the nearer it cometh to the New Moon, the better shall that year be. If it cometh when the moon decreaseth, it shall be a hard year, and the nearer the latter end thereof it cometh, the worse and harder shall the year be."

MOON WOOD

"Moon wood" is highly prized in Japan, Austria and southern Germany. Custom dictates that this wood comes from trees felled around Christmas during a waning moon. The felled tree is then dried out on the forest floor, with its top pointing downward for eight weeks. After cutting, the wood should rest for a further two years. For believers, the resulting moon wood is hardier and more suitable for carving.

— ☾ —

In Japan, the Horyuji Temple – the oldest wooden building in the world – was likely to have been built using traditional moon wood. Analysis of the central pillar of the pagoda estimates that the wood used was felled in 594 CE. For hundreds of years, Swiss artisans have been crafting world-renowned instruments using spruce from the Risoud Forest between France and Switzerland that's felled during a waning moon in the depths of winter.

— ☾ —

Believers claim that the moon's magnetic pull on the tree sap is weakest during the winter months, so harvested wood is dry, more durable and less prone to pests.

According to hearsay, the legendary violin maker Antonio Stradivari relied on moon wood for his famous Stradivarius instruments. Studies show he could have been barking up the right tree as they revealed that moon wood was indeed drier.

> ### *Did you know?*
>
> There is no such thing as the "dark side of the moon". The phrase refers to the side we never see. A more accurate term would be the far side of the moon.
>
> Because the moon is tidally locked to Earth – meaning it rotates on its axis at the same speed as it moves around Earth – we always see the same side. This movement is called synchronous rotation.

MARKINGS ON THE MOON

In Germanic cultures, the moon's markings are believed to depict an old woodcutter with a bundle of sticks. Legend has it that he was banished to the moon after being caught working on the Sabbath.

— ☾ —

In Hawaiian mythology, the moon shows a woman called Hina with a banyan tree. In New Zealand, Māori people see a captive maiden named Rona who disrespected the moon.

— ☾ —

Indian moon-gazers thought they could see the handprints of the *Astangi Mata* – the mother of all living things.

— ☾ —

Some Shi'ite Muslims believe that the pattern on the moon spells out the name of Ali, son-in-law of Muhammad.

DEFYING GRAVITY

Because the mass and size of an object determines its gravity, the surface gravity on the moon is about one-sixth of the surface gravity on Earth. Gravity affects weight, so even though a person's mass is the same on the moon, their experience of weight changes – this explains the pictures of astronauts seemingly leaping across the moon.

— ☾ —

While bouncing around looks fun, a long-term lack of gravity could have profound health implications. Scientists now believe the partial gravity on the moon wouldn't put enough weight on the body to protect it against loss of bone mass, muscle strength and heart-pumping capacity.

— ☾ —

Astronauts spending significant time in space have to exercise for hours every day to maintain musculoskeletal health – weightlifting, running and biking on resistance machines.

MOON MUSIC

Because the moon is in the vacuum of space, sound waves can't travel to or from it. However, in 1969, when astronauts on Apollo 10 passed by the dark side of the moon – the furthest point from Earth humans have ever been – they noticed strange unexplained sounds. In declassified audio transcripts released online by NASA in 2008 and audio files released in 2012, the astronauts discuss the sounds:

"That music even sounds outer-spacey, doesn't it," astronaut Eugene Cernan comments. *"You hear that? That whistling sound."*

"Boy, that sure is weird music." he comments later.

"We're going to have to find out about that," command module pilot, John Young, says. *"Nobody will believe us."*

At this point, the astronauts were far out of contact with Earth.

Scientists have since said that the sounds were likely to be radio interference, but conspiracy theories abound. In the recording, the astronauts discuss whether they should mention the sounds. They never publicly addressed the matter.

Do not swear by the moon, for she changes constantly. Then your love would also change.

WILLIAM SHAKESPEARE

FINAL WORD

Did you spot a young Crescent Moon in January? Or dodge showers thanks to signs from the moon in April? Perhaps you caught the dawn eclipse in May or basked in the glow of the Harvest Moon in September.

— ☾ —

Connecting with the moon throughout the seasons may have brought a sense of perspective to your life – a reminder that we're all part of something bigger than ourselves. Perhaps discovering the moon's role in culture, folklore and history felt unifying; we all see the same moon, no matter who we are or where we live. Following the moon's rhythms may have shone a light on the cyclical nature of life: just as the moon waxes and wanes, our daily existence – indeed, our entire human experience – is one of birth, growth, maturity and transformation.

So, whether you've enjoyed a year of moon bathing, or merely glimpsed her face in passing, know that the show isn't over. The moon cycle continues night after night, and there will always be a next time. Every 29.5 days brings a new New Moon. A Full Moon will always follow two weeks later. Our nearest satellite is standing by, whenever you feel the urge to connect. As expressed in Ecclesiastes 3:1, "There is a time for everything, and a season for every activity under the heavens."

FURTHER RESOURCES

Books

A Poem for Every Night of the Year, compiled by Allie Esiri

Lunar Living, by Kirsty Gallagher

Moonology: Working with the Magic of Lunar Cycles, by Yasmin Boland

National Trust: 2021 Nature Month-By-Month: A Children's Almanac by Anna Wilson

Red Moon, by Miranda Gray

Red Sky at Night: The Book of Lost Country Wisdom, by Jane Struthers

The Moon: A History for the Future, by Oliver Morton

The Natural Gardener: A Lifetime of Gardening by the Phases of the Moon, by John Harris and Jim Rickards

The Wise Wound, by Penelope Shuttle and Peter Redgrove

To The Moon: An Anthology Of Lunar Poems, by Carol Ann Duffy

Websites

timeanddate.com/astronomy

moon.nasa.gov

skyatnightmagazine.com

almanac.com

cafeastrology.com/whats-my-moon-sign.html

mirandagray.co.uk

uk.rhythmofnature.net

If you're interested in finding out more about our books, find us on Facebook at **Summersdale Publishers**, on Twitter at **@Summersdale** and on Instagram at **@Summersdalebooks**.

www.summersdale.com